Pets and People

Bernard J. Weiss
Senior Author
Reading and Linguistics

Susan B. Cruikshank
Reading and Language Arts

Eldonna L. Evertts
Language Arts

Loreli Olson Steuer
Reading and Linguistics

Lyman C. Hunt
General Editor—Satellite Books

Holt
Basic
Reading

Level 5

HOLT, RINEHART AND WINSTON, PUBLISHERS
New York • Toronto • Mexico City • London • Sydney • Tokyo

ISBN 0-03-061386-8
789 071 7654

Acknowledgments:

Grateful acknowledgment is given to G. P. Putnam's Sons for "The Goldfish," from *Everything and Anything* by Dorothy Aldis. Copyright 1925, 1926, 1927 by Dorothy Aldis. Used by permission.

Art Credits:

Ethel Gold, pages 4 – 11
Jerry Zimmerman, pages 12 – 21
Len Ebert, pages 22 – 29
Marilyn Bass Goldman, page 30
Carolyn Bracken, page 31
Lorraine Fox, pages 32 – 40
Diane de Groat, pages 41, 52 – 61
Tom Tierney, pages 42 – 50
Kathleen Allert, page 51
Viewpoint Graphics, Inc., page 62
Cover art by James Endicott

Table of Contents

4

Stop Gus!

Gus ran into a big store.

Sandy ran into the store.

Gus and Sandy ran into the store.

"Stop, Gus!

Stop, Gus," she said.

Gus didn't stop.

A big boy saw Gus.

"Stop," the big boy said.
"Come here, dog."

Gus didn't stop.
He ran out.

Two girls saw Gus.
"Stop," the two girls said.

The girls ran to stop Gus.
Gus didn't stop.

A little boy saw Gus.

"Here, dog," said the little boy.
"Come here. Good dog.
See the cookies?"

Gus saw the cookies.

What did he do?

He ran to the little boy.

The big boy and the girls saw Gus.

What did they do?

They ran to Gus and the boy.

Sandy didn't stop Gus.

The big boy didn't stop Gus.

The two girls didn't stop Gus.

The little boy didn't stop Gus.

The cookies did!

A Good Game

A bear ran and ran.

The bear saw a little pig.

"Come and play," said the bear.

"Do what I do.

It is a good game.

It is fun to play."

The bear ran and ran.

And the pig ran and ran.

The bear came to the water.

Into the water went the bear.

And into the water went the pig.

The bear went down in the water.

And the pig went down in the water.

Up came the bear.

And up came the pig.

Out went the bear.

And out went the pig.

The bear and the pig ran and ran.

They saw a cow.

The bear said, "Come and play, cow.

Do what I do.

It is a good game.

It is fun to play."

The bear and the pig ran.

And the cow ran.

They came to a store.

The bear went into the store.

The pig went into the store.

And the cow went into the store.

Someone said, "Look!"

Someone said, "Help, help!"

Someone said, "Get out! Get out!"

The bear and the pig ran out.

And the cow ran out.

The bear and the pig and the cow ran.

They saw a dog.

The bear said, "Come and play, dog.

Do what I do.

It is a good game.

It is fun to play."

The bear and the pig and the cow ran.
And the dog ran.

They came to a house.
It was a little house.
It was good for one bear.

The bear ran into the house.

"Stop!" said the bear.

"Do **not** do what I do.

Do **not** come in.

The house is good for one bear.

"Good-by, dog and cow.

Good-by, pig.

The game was fun!"

Swim Up!

"A kite!" said Sora.
"A kite like a goldfish!
What a good kite!
Is it for me?"

Sora saw a sign on the kite.

The sign said,

To Sora

From Big Brother

The kite was from Big Brother!

Big Brother was in Japan.

"Swim, goldfish," said Sora.

"Swim in the sky.

Swim up.

Swim up in the sky."

The goldfish went up.
Up in the sky it went.

And up went Sora!

"Good-by, house!" said Sora.
"Good-by!
My goldfish likes to swim up in the sky!"

"I see a house!" said Sora.

"It **is** a house," said the kite.
"A house in Japan!"

"I see a boy," said Sora.
"Is he my brother?
He is my brother
in Japan!"

"Goldfish, what a trick!" said Sora.
"My goldfish can swim in the sky.
My goldfish can swim to Japan.
I like my goldfish from Japan!"

"What a kite!" said Big Brother.

"What a Sora!" said the kite.

The Goldfish

My darling little goldfish
Hasn't any toes;
He swims around without a sound
And bumps his hungry nose.

He can't get out to play with me,
Nor I get in to him,
Although I say: "Come out and play,"
And he—"Come in and swim."

—Dorothy Aldis

Making New Words

ran	it	did	up	can
rag	if	dig	us	cat

Gus ran with the rag.

Sora can find the cat.

See us up here.

Did Rex like to dig?

Sandy will read it if she can.

Final Consonant Substitution. Have each pair of words read, calling attention to the final consonant substitution in the second word. Then have the sentences read.

Shep, the Sheep Dog

Shep was a sheep dog.

He was a good sheep dog.

"Come here, Shep!" said Tim.

Shep came.

"My little sheep is not here," said Tim.

"Go find it, Shep."

Shep went to find the little sheep.

He saw the little sheep.

The sheep ran and ran.

Shep ran and ran.

The little sheep came to the water.

The little sheep went into the water.

Shep came to the water.

Shep went into the water.

He went in to get the sheep.

Tim ran to find Shep.

Shep was in the water.

The little sheep was in the water.

"Come out, Shep," said Tim.

"Make the little sheep come out."

The little sheep came out.

Shep came out.

They came out from the water.

"Good dog," said Tim.

"My dog is a good sheep dog."

Stringing Words

Get	three	signs.
Make	two	books.
Read	the	games.
Find		
See		

Did	Gus	get	three	signs?
Can	Sandy	make	two	books?
	Tim	read	the	games?
	Jenny	find		
		see		

41

The Cow

A little boy was in the house.

"I want to play," he said.

"I will get my brother."

The little boy ran to get his brother.

"Play with me," said the little boy.

"No," said his brother.

"I do not want to play.

I want to play with my dog."

The little boy saw a big girl.

"Play with me," he said.

"No," said the girl.

"I do not want to play.

I want to read my book."

"What can I do?" asked the little boy.

The little boy saw a cow.

He ran to the cow.

"I will make the cow play," he said.

And up on the cow he went.

"Get up, cow," said the boy.

"Get up and play with me.
Get up and go."

The cow did not go.

"The cow will not get up," said the boy.
"The cow will not play."

The big girl saw the little boy.

"Come down," said the girl.
"The cow will not go."

"What can a cow do?"
asked the boy.

"See," said the girl.

"Here is what a cow can do."

The Cow

The friendly cow all red and white,

I love with all my heart:

She gives me cream

    with all her might,

To eat with apple tart.

—Robert Louis Stevenson

Who Is It?

A little girl went to see Kolo.
She went to his house.

"Kolo, Kolo," she said.
"Come out and play."

"Who is it?" asked someone.

"It is Neko," said the girl.
"I want to play with Kolo."

"Who is it?" asked someone again.

"Neko," said the girl.

"I want Kolo to come out."

"Who is it?" asked someone.

"It is Neko," said the girl again.

"Get Kolo for me.

I want to play with Kolo."

Neko saw Kolo come to the house.

"Kolo," said Neko.
"Come and play with me.
Who is in the house?"

"No one is in the house," said Kolo.

"Someone asked, 'Who is it?'
Someone **is** in the house," said Neko.

"Come with me," said Kolo.

"Come in and see who it is."

Kolo and Neko went into the house.

"Someone **is** here," said Kolo.

"And here he is!"

Putting Words Together

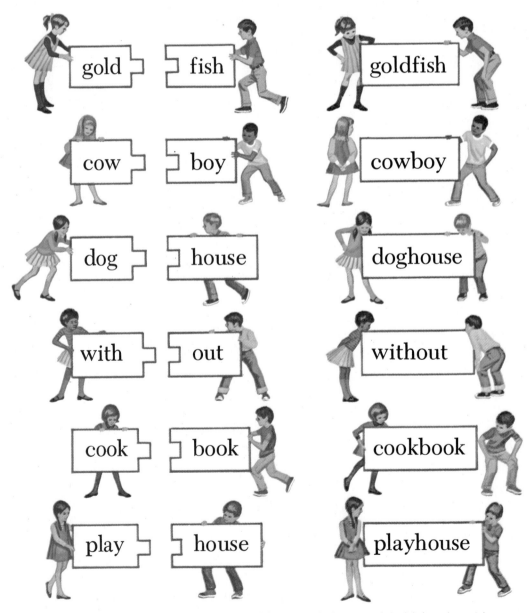

gold	fish	goldfish
cow	boy	cowboy
dog	house	doghouse
with	out	without
cook	book	cookbook
play	house	playhouse

Compound Words. Have children read the word held by the girl and the word held by the boy. Then have the compound word read.

Stringing Words

Jenny		
The girl	likes	games.
She		

Jim and Don		
The boys	make	cookies.
They		

Tim		
The boy	sees	someone.
He		

Meg and Sandy		
The girls	play	here.
They		

Sentence Patterns. Have the children choose a word or words from each column to form sentences.

New Words

The words listed beside the page numbers below are introduced in *Pets and People*, Level 5 in the HOLT BASIC READING SERIES. The words printed in italics are easily decoded.

5. stop	16. cow	33. Shep
Gus	18. someone	sheep
6. *ran*	*get*	35. *Tim*
Sandy	20. was	44. want
didn't	23. swim	*will*
7. saw	24. *kite*	his
he	Sora	45. *no*
boy	goldfish	with
10. what	25. brother	46. *girl*
12. *it*	Japan	47. asked
I	from	53. who
13. *came*	26. sky	54. Kolo
water	27. my	Neko
went	29. *can*	56. again